GW01246578

Original title:
Frozen Stars

Copyright © 2024 Swan Charm
All rights reserved.

Author: Kaido Väinamäe
ISBN HARDBACK: 978-9916-79-711-2
ISBN PAPERBACK: 978-9916-79-712-9
ISBN EBOOK: 978-9916-79-713-6

Cosmic Silence

In the dark expanse, stars softly gleam,
Whispers of silence weave a dream.
Galaxies swirl in a peaceful dance,
Time drifts away in a cosmic trance.

Nebulae bloom in colors so bright,
Veils of mystery engulf the night.
Planets spin gently on paths unknown,
Embracing the vastness, utterly alone.

The void holds secrets, a soothing hush,
Echoes of stardust in a gentle rush.
Where light years meld in heavenly grace,
Silence surrounds this boundless space.

In weaves of gravity, beauty takes flight,
Wonders unfold in the stillness of night.
Cosmic songs, sung in ethereal tones,
Softly remind us, we're never alone.

So gaze at the heavens, let your heart soar,
Embrace the silence, forever explore.
In the cosmic sea, where dreams intertwine,
Find peace in the stillness, let your soul shine.

Celestial Crystals

In the night sky, stars ignite,
Crystals shimmering, pure and bright.
Whispers of dreams dance in air,
A cosmic ballet, beyond compare.

Fragments of light, a woven thread,
Painting the heavens, where wishes tread.
Every twinkle tells a tale,
Of love and loss, of hope's own sail.

Chilled Luminescence

Under the moon's soft, silver glow,
Chilled luminescence starts to flow.
Night's gentle breath upon the sea,
Whispers secrets, setting hearts free.

Frosted patterns on windowpanes,
Nature's artwork, beauty remains.
Each glimmering flake, a fleeting spark,
Guides our journey through the dark.

Frigid Constellations

Frigid constellations in the sky,
Silent stories as they pass by.
Each star a beacon, shining clear,
A map of dreams for us to steer.

Frozen whispers of the ancient night,
Illuminate paths with their silver light.
Boundless wonders to behold,
Timeless tales in silence told.

Ethereal Glimmers

Ethereal glimmers in the dawn,
Awakening life as night is gone.
Soft light dances on dew-kissed grass,
Moments fleeting, never to last.

Whispers of dawn, so sweet and clear,
Nature's chorus that we hold dear.
Each ray a promise, a brand new start,
Binding us close, heart to heart.

Twinkling Icebergs

In the night, they gleam bright,
Silent giants, vast and white.
Underneath the starlit sky,
Whispers of the cold winds sigh.

Cracks and creaks, a subtle sound,
Floating dreams, where dreams surround.
Each glimmer holds a story old,
Secrets in the ice, tales untold.

Majestic forms in the moonlight dance,
Nature's magic, a fleeting chance.
Reflecting stars on crystal clear,
Frosty splendor, drawing near.

Waves embrace in softest grace,
Ethereal forms in a quiet space.
Carved by time and nature's hand,
A frozen world, so grand and planned.

In the quiet, stillness grows,
Amidst the pale, the beauty flows.
Twinkling icebergs kiss the sea,
A shimmering sight, wild and free.

Paintings of the Cosmos

Upon the night, colors swirl,
Galaxy's canvas begins to unfurl.
Stars, like brushstrokes in the dark,
A portrait of light, a vivid spark.

Nebulas bloom in hues so bright,
A celestial dance, pure delight.
Each dot a story, vast and clear,
Whispers of worlds that feel so near.

Comets trail with a shimmering tail,
Chasing dreams through the cosmic veil.
Planets spin in graceful ballet,
Lost in the art of night and day.

Constellations weave through the space,
In patterns formed, a cosmic lace.
Every heartbeat, a tune unknown,
In this gallery, we're never alone.

Beyond horizons, where wonders lie,
Galactic visions, far and nigh.
Each painting whispers of what might be,
A tapestry of the great infinity.

Frosted Imagination

In the hush of winter nights,
Dreams take flight in frosty sights.
Whispers dance on chilly air,
Imagination blooms everywhere.

Snowflakes swirl, a silent song,
Painting visions all night long.
Children laugh, their spirits soar,
Magic grows with tales of yore.

Crystal castles, worlds anew,
Within the heart, a vibrant hue.
Winter's breath brings life to dreams,
Frosted hopes, like silver beams.

Every flake an artist's touch,
Crafting wonder, oh so much.
A canvas white, pure and wide,
Frosted imagination as our guide.

In the cold, our hearts ignite,
Creating warmth, a spark of light.
In this frozen, vivid scene,
Dreams unfold where we've all been.

Distant Glows

In the twilight, shadows play,
Distant glows guide the way.
Faintly flickering, stars align,
Across the vast, an endless sign.

Whispers travel through the air,
Calling softly, a distant flare.
Like lanterns sailing in the night,
They beckon forth with gentle light.

Across the hills, they paint the sky,
Guiding wanderers who pass by.
Each glow a promise, hope in store,
A pathway open, forever more.

In quiet moments, hearts can see,
The warmth of light that sets us free.
Distance fades, the dream ignites,
In the silence, we find our sights.

So follow onwards, let it show,
Embrace the magic of distant glow.
For in each gleam, we find our place,
In the cosmos, a warm embrace.

Ethereal Sparkle

In twilight's hush, soft whispers play,
The fireflies dance, as night meets day.
Gentle glows weave through the trees,
Carried on the cool, refreshing breeze.

Dreams take flight on silken wings,
In the stillness, the heart firmly clings.
To starlit paths where shadows blend,
Ethereal sparkle, our souls ascend.

Luminous tales of yesteryear,
In vivid hues, our visions clear.
With every flicker, hope ignites,
A galaxy blooms in the darkest nights.

Glistening Cold Horizons

Beyond the hills, where the cold winds sigh,
Crystal landscapes stretch and lie.
Every breath, a frosty mist,
Hidden wonders, too sweet to resist.

Mountains rise with glistening crowns,
Wrapped in white, nature frowns.
The sun's embrace, a distant glow,
Kisses the earth where silence grows.

Footsteps crunch on the frozen ground,
Whispers of winter's magic abound.
With every sight, a tale unfolds,
Of glistening dreams in the biting cold.

The Silent Night's Embrace

In the quiet, shadows softly creep,
While the world lies in tranquil sleep.
Stars hang low, a celestial quilt,
Wrapped in peace, all worries stilled.

The moonlight pours like silvery wine,
Over landscapes, both yours and mine.
Every twinkling light above,
Calls forth those whispers of love.

Crickets chirp their lullabies,
Underneath the vast, velvet skies.
A tapestry of dreams we weave,
In the silent night, we believe.

Stars Caught in Snowflakes

As snowflakes fall, a dance of fate,
Each one unique, we contemplate.
Starlit wishes on gentle white,
Illuminate our hearts' delight.

In the hush of winter's fold,
Secrets of the universe told.
Every shimmer, a glimmering spark,
A universe hidden in the dark.

We trace the paths where the starlight beams,
In the quiet moment, we share our dreams.
Caught in the wonder, our spirits soar,
Stars caught in snowflakes, forevermore.

Cosmic Hues of Winter

In the stillness of the night,
Stars twinkle, a serene sight.
Frosted whispers fill the air,
Under the moon's gentle stare.

Silver clouds drift softly by,
Painting dreams across the sky.
A blanket of snow, pure and bright,
Guides the heart towards the light.

Echoes of laughter in the cold,
Stories of warmth yet untold.
Winter's breath in every hue,
Colors the world in a tranquil view.

Trees adorned with icy lace,
Nature's art in perfect grace.
As the universe sways and spins,
Within winter's chill, warmth begins.

Cosmic dance of dark and light,
In winter's arms, everything feels right.
With each step on the snowy floor,
The heart finds peace forevermore.

Polar Constellations

Above the tundra, where silence reigns,
Stars ignite in jewel-studded chains.
The sky unfolds its ancient map,
A cosmic quilt in winter's lap.

Auroras swirl in vivid streams,
Shattering darkness with vibrant dreams.
Beneath their glow, the landscape sighs,
As icy winds whisper winter's cries.

Each point of light, a distant sun,
Guiding travelers, one by one.
Frozen whispers of the night,
Embrace the world in shimmering light.

With every breath, the chill descends,
Nature's symphony, as stillness bends.
In the vastness where shadows meet,
Polar stars sing, calm and sweet.

Resting under this celestial dome,
The heart feels quiet, the spirit roams.
Amongst the constellations bred,
In frozen stillness, lives are led.

Glinting Coldness

Amidst the frost, stark and bright,
Glinting shards in the pale moonlight.
Every breath a cloud, pure and clear,
Whispers of winter, drawing near.

Crystalline paths where shadows creep,
Echoes of secrets the night will keep.
The world is hushed, a soft embrace,
In glinting coldness, time finds grace.

A dance of snowflakes, free and wild,
Nature's wonder, innocent and mild.
Each flake a treasure, unique and rare,
Falling gently, with tender care.

Frost-kissed branches, a glittering sight,
Sway softly in the veils of night.
In the stillness, a magical hold,
Wrapped in the warmth of glinting cold.

As morning breaks, the sun will rise,
Bathing the world in golden ties.
Yet in the heart, winter will stay,
In glinting coldness, forever play.

Nebula's Breath

In the dark expanse, a nebula spins,
Breath of creation where starlight begins.
Colors unfurl in a cosmic mist,
Whispers of galaxies that cannot resist.

With every pulse, the universe sighs,
Cradling secrets amidst the skies.
Veils of stardust, glowing and bright,
Envelop the world in a tapestry of light.

Nebula's breath, a gentle embrace,
Stirring the stillness of quiet space.
In the silence, new worlds are born,
Woven into the fabric of dawn.

Stars emerge from the cosmic womb,
Dancing through the ever-expanding gloom.
In this cradle of celestial lore,
Nebula's breath opens the door.

As we gaze at the endless night,
We find our place in the cosmic flight.
Boundless wonder in every thread,
In nebula's breath, our spirits are fed.

Crystalline Nightscape

Under the dark canopy, stars gleam bright,
Whispers of the cosmos, a dazzling sight.
Moonbeams dance softly on the frozen lake,
Nature's own marvel, a dream to awake.

Shadows of trees cast a mystical air,
Each crystal flake sparkles, beyond compare.
Silence wraps gently, like a warm embrace,
In this serene moment, we find our place.

The night unfolds secrets, to hearts that will hear,
A symphony soft, from the skies so clear.
Constellations twinkle, stories they weave,
In the crystalline landscape, we dare to believe.

Luminescent Frost

Morning arrives with a glistening coat,
Frost on the branches, a delicate note.
Sunlight ignites the ice into fire,
Each crystal shimmering, a sight to admire.

Breath of the earth, wrapped in winter's chill,
Nature's embrace whispers, quiet and still.
Every step crinkles like dreams in the dawn,
Awakening wonders from twilight withdrawn.

Pale shades of blue blend with golden rays,
A dance of frost's magic in shimmering displays.
Life's gentle rhythm, both tranquil and bright,
In this luminescent world, pure delight.

Silent Stellar Symphony

In the night's hush, a melody flows,
Stars play their notes, as a soft wind blows.
Galaxies twirl in an endless embrace,
Creating a rhythm, a cosmic grace.

Celestial whispers weave through the air,
A harmony of stillness, beyond all care.
Each twinkle a chord, in the vastness they sing,
Unraveling secrets that starlight may bring.

Constellations twinkle, a visual tune,
Painting the heavens with dreams of the moon.
In this silent symphony, hope takes flight,
Boundless and free in the canvas of night.

Veil of White Light

A soft shroud of mist blankets the ground,
In silence, the world wraps in beauty profound.
Morning breaks gently, with whispers so bright,
Kissing the earth with a veil of white light.

Glistening petals, draped in dew's grace,
Each moment unfolds in this tranquil space.
Nature's embrace, warm as a sigh,
Filling the heart as the shadows pass by.

Birds stir from slumber in vibrant display,
Choruses rise as the night slips away.
Life awakens slowly, like dawn's gentle flight,
Wrapped in the glow of a veil, pure and bright.

Celestial Glacier

In the hush of night, it gleams,
A shimmering veil, frozen dreams.
Beneath the stars, a silver sheen,
Nature's masterpiece, serene.

Rivers of ice, they twist and flow,
Carving paths in the soft, white glow.
Each crystal spark, a twinkling light,
Guides the heart through the frozen night.

Echoes whisper on chilly winds,
Stories of love that the quiet sends.
Shadows dance on the frozen ground,
Where ancient echoes softly sound.

A timeless realm, where silence reigns,
In the stillness, there's no more pain.
Embraced by winter's cool embrace,
We find our peace in this sacred space.

Celestial wonders draw our gaze,
As we drift in a tranquil daze.
Amidst the glimmer, hopes take flight,
In the heart of this icy night.

Frigid Twilight

At dusk when shadows start to creep,
The world grows hushed, the air runs deep.
Colors fade into a soft gray,
As daylight gently slips away.

Chilled winds whisper, secrets kept,
While twilight's grip, the silence swept.
Stars emerge in the cobalt sky,
Winking softly as time drifts by.

Frigid moments, crisp and clear,
Breath turns to mist, drawing near.
Nature's palette, stark and bold,
Paints the stories yet untold.

A hush descends, the night unfolds,
Wrapping the earth in jeweled folds.
Here in the dark, dreams take flight,
In the embrace of the frigid night.

Reflections shimmer on frozen streams,
Carrying forth our silent dreams.
In frigid twilight, we find our way,
Guided by stars till break of day.

Starry Ice

Across the lake, a mirror bright,
Captures the dance of stars at night.
Each twinkle rests on glacial plains,
Where the heart knows no more pains.

Whispers float on the icy breath,
Echoes of life, even in death.
Reflections speak in silent tones,
Under the canopy of stones.

Moonlight casts a ghostly glow,
Over the fields of glimmer and snow.
Each flake a wish, a timeless prayer,
Carried forth through the cold night air.

In frozen stillness, all is calm,
The world cradled in a gentle balm.
Time stands still, lost in desire,
As we walk on paths of ice and fire.

Starry dreams on a frosted sea,
Guide us home, set our spirits free.
In this realm of night's embrace,
We find our joy, our perfect place.

Polestar Reveries

Under the watch of the polestar bright,
Dreamers gather in the still of night.
Guided by light that pierces the dark,
Each heart ignites with a hopeful spark.

In reveries woven with cosmic threads,
Whispers of peace dance in our heads.
Lost in thoughts, as soft winds sigh,
We reach for dreams that linger high.

Across the vastness, we navigate,
Finding solace in a shared fate.
Stars entwined, stories to share,
In the comfort of night, without a care.

With every breath, a promise made,
In the glow of dreams, we are not afraid.
Polestar leading our way to dawn,
Embracing the beauty we build upon.

So let us wander through night's embrace,
In the reveries, we find our place.
Under the sky, forever true,
We dance with stars, me and you.

Glimmering Subzero

In the hush of a midnight sky,
Stars twinkle, quietly nigh,
Snowflakes dance in gentle grace,
Nature's beauty, a soft embrace.

Icy breath in the still of the night,
Whispers echo, pure delight,
Moonbeams spin a silver thread,
Through the dreams of those long dead.

Crystal worlds beneath my feet,
Winter's wonder, oh so sweet,
Glimmers bright on branches bare,
Subzero magic fills the air.

Frosty patterns draw the eye,
Nature's art that can't deny,
Each moment a fleeting treasure,
Chilling us with endless pleasure.

As dawn approaches, light unfolds,
A palette rich with azure golds,
Yet in the quiet, I will keep,
The secrets of the night so deep.

Fractal Frost

Nature's fingers paint the trees,
Fractal frost in gentle breeze,
Each crystal holds a thousand dreams,
Winter's canvas, or so it seems.

Patterns dance, both small and grand,
Woven whispers across the land,
Each flake unique, a fleeting sigh,
In the stillness, time goes by.

Echoes of a chill embrace,
Cascading light, a soft lace,
Snowflakes flutter, softly fall,
Fractals etched, nature's call.

In each moment, coldness sings,
Underneath the weight of wings,
Silent tales on icy breath,
Frosted memories of death.

But in this cold, there's life anew,
Healing layers cloaked in hue,
Fractal whispers in the night,
Promising warmth with morning light.

Nebulous Chills

In shadows cast by frigid air,
Nebulous chills everywhere,
Whirling mists of silver sigh,
Drift like whispers, drift on high.

Frosted veins in nature's flow,
Caught in the dance of ice and snow,
Silent echoes fill the night,
While stars above shine cold and bright.

Crisp breath plucks at hidden dreams,
Veils of winter's gentle schemes,
Ghostly shapes in moonlit haze,
Softly calling through the days.

As twilight falls, the world stands still,
Chills embrace with quiet thrill,
In the mystery of every flake,
Nature's secret dreams awake.

With whispers lost in midnight's lure,
These nebulous chills, so pure,
A fragile world wrapped in cold,
Stories of winter delicately told.

Aurora's Silence

In the quiet of the polar night,
Auroras dance, a ghostly light,
Colors weave through vast expanse,
In a spellbinding, fleeting trance.

Beneath the glow, the world is hushed,
Where dreams and reality are brushed,
Softly glowing, the sky ignites,
In the mystery of dazzling sights.

Stars recede in rhythmic sway,
As the colors bend and play,
Each flicker tells a tale untold,
Of ancient magic strong and bold.

A crisp chill fills the empty space,
As nature dons her velvet grace,
In silence, all the creatures gaze,
Captivated by this glowing haze.

Time stands still in this sacred dance,
Under the aurora's mystic glance,
Wrapped in beauty's soft embrace,
A moment caught in timeless space.

Frozen Radiance

In the stillness of the night,
Crystals gleam, pure and bright.
Moonlight dances on the lake,
Whispers soft, the silence quake.

Frozen trees in silver light,
Branches sparkle, an icy sight.
Footsteps crunch on frosted ground,
Nature's magic, beauty found.

Stars above in tranquil grace,
Guide the wanderers in this place.
Cold winds sing a haunting tune,
Beneath the watchful, brightened moon.

A blanket white, serene and vast,
Captures echoes of the past.
Time stands still in frost's embrace,
In this realm, a sacred space.

Emerald leaves and flowers freeze,
Were once vibrant in the breeze.
Yet in cold, they find their form,
A frozen art in life's great storm.

Celestial Frost

Veils of frost in dawn's first light,
Dreams awaken, take their flight.
In a world where silence reigns,
Whispers glide on crystal chains.

Stars are dressed in coats of white,
Dancing through the velvet night.
Each breath clouds the freezing air,
In this beauty, hearts lay bare.

Frozen rivers seem to flow,
In their depths, the moonlight glows.
Nature's canvas brushed so neat,
Whispers secret, soft and sweet.

With each flake that tumbles down,
Nature's crown, a silver gown.
Magic breathes in every frost,
In these moments, time is lost.

Beneath the weight of winter's kiss,
Lies a world of tranquil bliss.
In the chill, we find our peace,
As the frozen whispers cease.

Eclipsed by Ice

Shadows creep on icy trails,
Echoes whisper, faintly wails.
Branches bend beneath the weight,
Silent screams of winter's fate.

Eclipsed by cold, the world feels small,
Underneath a snow-draped pall.
Each step forward, careful, slow,
Through the fields where silence grows.

Darkened skies and swirling snow,
Swallowed whole by winter's glow.
Stars hide behind a shroud of grey,
In the stillness, dreams decay.

Yet within this frozen plight,
Glimmers of unseen light.
Hope emerges from the frost,
In this beauty, never lost.

Nature's depths, a quiet hymn,
Life persists, though edges dim.
With each breath, a spark remains,
Eclipsed by ice, yet life sustains.

The Icebound Canvas

Nature paints with frozen hues,
Every whisper tells the news.
Blanket white on every tree,
A masterpiece for all to see.

Frozen lakes like glass reflect,
Heaven's beauty, perfect and direct.
Footprints left without a trace,
In the stillness, hearts embrace.

Each flake falls, a work of art,
Crafted gently, nature's heart.
Time suspends in frosted grace,
Life and love in this cold space.

As shadows lengthen, daylight fades,
Colors shift in winter's shades.
The world transforms into a dream,
On the icebound canvas, schemes.

With every layer, life renews,
In this realm of sacred views.
Winter's breath, a silent muse,
In its chill, the heart will choose.

Celestial Frostbite

Stars whisper secrets low,
In the icy night's glow.
Frozen breaths in the air,
A chill from dreams laid bare.

Moonlight drapes the still earth,
As silence hums its birth.
Each flake a tale untold,
In silver hues, bold and cold.

The cosmos holds its breath,
In this dance, life and death.
Frosted paths, hidden tracks,
Guiding souls, none turn back.

Winds carry sighs through space,
A frozen, haunting grace.
Crystals sparkle and twinkle,
In starlight, destinies sink low.

Under this vast expanse,
Hearts caught in a trance.
Celestial frost, so tight,
Keeps us tethered through the night.

Diamonds in the Void

In the endless, dark abyss,
Tiny points of light kiss.
Each a dream, a shining ghost,
Whispers of the past we host.

Beyond the shadows of despair,
They gleam with beauty rare.
Wonders linger in the gloom,
Birth new worlds with every bloom.

Galaxies spin, faint and bright,
Fading in the endless night.
Yet diamonds blink through the black,
Giving hope, refusing lack.

Secrets dance in the vastness,
In stillness, find their vastness.
With every spark, a wish reborn,
In the void, a heart can mourn.

Like lost souls finding their peace,
In the dark, they seek release.
Diamonds in the void shine long,
Where silence sings its soft song.

Whispering Glaciers

Ancient giants stand so tall,
Cradling secrets, they call.
Voices drift on the cold air,
Echoes of a time laid bare.

Underneath the dazzling sheen,
Stories linger, rarely seen.
Each crack tells a tale of old,
In the silence, wisdom unfolds.

Flowing softly, ice and stone,
Whispering truths we once known.
With every shift, they reveal,
The history of time, surreal.

In the embrace of twilight's breath,
They stand strong against cold death.
Guardians of the earth's own heart,
From their majesty, we won't part.

With each thaw, new life shall start,
In frozen realms, warmth imparts.
Whispering glaciers, strong and wise,
Hold the past beneath the skies.

Nightfall's Crystals

As daylight fades, shadows creep,
Crystals burst, secrets to keep.
Twinkling in the dusky light,
Glimmers spark the coming night.

Branches lace with frost so fine,
Painting shapes through silence divine.
The world wears a cloak of dreams,
In the darkness, time redeems.

Whispers echo in the chill,
Stars align, the night stands still.
Each crystal holds a story bright,
Glistening stars, a pure delight.

Moonbeams sprinkle silver dust,
In this twilight, we must trust.
Nightfall's art, so clear, profound,
Magic in the stillness found.

As dusk softly takes its hold,
Crystals shimmer, young and old.
In the quiet, wonders bloom,
Guided by the moon's soft gloom.

Dankest Sky

In shadows deep, the night unfolds,
Whispers of dreams in silence told.
Stars blink faint in the heavy gloom,
While secrets lurk in the darkened room.

Clouds drift slow, like thoughts confined,
A chill creeps in, to hearts aligned.
Thunder grumbles, a distant sigh,
Underneath the dankest sky.

The moon peeks shy, a ghostly light,
Casting ghosts into the night.
With every breeze, the shadows dance,
In this twilight's haunting trance.

Echoes linger, time stretches wide,
Embracing fears, where phantoms hide.
In the stillness, we call, we cry,
For solace beneath this dankest sky.

Yet hope survives in whispers small,
In silence waiting, we hear the call.
With every dawn, the dark must die,
Renewing life beneath the sky.

Cosmic Slumber

In vastness deep, we drift and sway,
Stars like dreams, in night's ballet.
Gravity's pull, we float and glide,
In cosmic slumber, we abide.

Galaxies swirl, a dance divine,
In velvet darkness, we intertwine.
Stardust kisses, soft as sighs,
In endless nights, where wonder lies.

Comets blaze through time and space,
A fleeting glimpse of deep embrace.
Dreams awaken with each bright flare,
In this slumber, we find our share.

Nebulas cradle, colors bloom,
In cosmic folds, we chase the gloom.
The universe hums a lullaby,
As we lose ourselves in the sky.

Through silence vast, our spirits soar,
A journey boundless, forevermore.
In the depths of night, we fly high,
Wrapped in whispers of the cosmic sky.

Seraphic Ice

In crystal realms, where stillness reigns,
A world adorned with glistening chains.
Whispers echo through frosty air,
In the chill, serenity's rare.

Icicles dangle like delicate dreams,
Reflecting light in fractured beams.
Each flake a note in a silent song,
Where nature's beauty lingers long.

The frozen breath of a wintry night,
Wraps us gently in purest light.
Seraphic forms in the snow appear,
Guardians of peace, they draw us near.

Beneath the stars, the world feels tight,
Each breath a cloud in the tranquil night.
In this stillness, our hearts ignite,
Finding warmth in the seraphic light.

As dawn approaches, ice starts to weep,
Awakening life from its frozen sleep.
Yet in the chill, forever lies,
The sacred charm of seraphic ice.

Iced Elegance

A shimmer falls on winter's dress,
Nature cloaked in soft finesse.
Trees wear coats of frosted lace,
In iced elegance, they find their grace.

Ponds mirror skies of slate and grey,
A stillness holds, as if to say,
Time whispers secrets, soft and low,
In every flake, a tale to know.

Footprints trace the paths we tread,
With every step, a memory led.
In the crisp air, our laughter sings,
Bound by the beauty that winter brings.

Glimmers dance on the twilight's breath,
Chilled by the kiss of approaching death.
Yet warmth ignites in hearts we share,
In the elegance, we find our care.

As sunset drapes the world in gold,
Stories of warmth in peace retold.
In winter's grasp, our spirits rise,
To celebrate love beneath cold skies.

Mystical Frigid Visions

In the stillness of night, whispers glide,
Frosty dreams in a world wide.
Shimmering echoes dance in the air,
A tapestry woven with care.

Silent shadows play in the moon's embrace,
Glistening flakes in a cosmic chase.
Each breath taken, a cloud of frost,
In this realm, no warmth is lost.

Deep in the heart of winter's reign,
A kingdom of ice, untouched by pain.
Silent wishes drift like snow,
Lighting the paths where spirits flow.

Glimmers of magic in a frigid haze,
Wonders unfold in the longest days.
Timeless tales of love and lore,
Awake in dreams, eternally to explore.

Through the frost, the vision grows bright,
Chasing shadows into the light.
Mystical realms in a crystal cocoon,
Whispering secrets beneath the moon.

Celestial Crystals

Stars twinkle softly, like crystals formed,
In the night sky where wishes are warmed.
Glistening beads of cosmic grace,
Illuminate the void, a vast embrace.

Amongst the wonders, the starlight glows,
Lights that shimmer, a dance that flows.
Each crystal formed in a cosmic stream,
Reflects our hopes, each one a dream.

A tapestry woven from stardust's thread,
Whispering tales of the long-gone dead.
Each shard a glimpse into timeless fate,
Celestial patterns that we contemplate.

In the silent depths, a spark ignites,
Awakening visions through tranquil nights.
Celestial prisms burst into sight,
With every heartbeat, they take flight.

Boundless skies filled with shimmering hues,
Echoing secrets in celestial clues.
A universe crafted from crystalline lore,
Opens the heart to forever explore.

Chilling Constellations

Beneath the veil of midnight's glow,
Chilly stars twinkle, a cosmic show.
Patterns emerge in the air so cold,
Stories of ancient worlds, bold.

In the depths of the cosmic seas,
Constellations whisper through the breeze.
Sculpted shapes with a tale to share,
Connect the dots with a loving care.

Frozen wonders in the starlit night,
Each point of light a guiding sight.
Chilling patterns in a velvet sky,
Inviting dreams that soar and fly.

Drifting through the celestial dance,
Under the enchantment of night's romance.
With every glance, the heart's embraced,
By chilling constellations, interlaced.

Glimmers of hope in the distant scheme,
Painting a picture of every dream.
Guided by stars, we navigate still,
Chilling constellations, infinite thrill.

Icy Lightyears

In the silence of space, light-years unfold,
Icy breezes carry tales untold.
Travel the cosmos, where seasons bend,
In the arms of the universe, dreams transcend.

Frosted whispers echo through the void,
Each journey taken, a path enjoyed.
Across galaxies, the cold winds weave,
Icy truths hidden, we dare to believe.

Stars, like diamonds, in darkness gleam,
Painting the night with a silvery dream.
Time stretches thin as we venture far,
In the realm of ice, beneath each star.

Infinity beckons with shimmering hue,
An icy embrace awaits for you.
Through light-years traveled, the heart remains,
Bound to the cosmos where magic reigns.

In this expanse, we find our peace,
Icy revelations that never cease.
A voyage through time, both distant and near,
In icy lightyears, all dreams endear.

Shimmering Nightfall

As twilight whispers softly near,
The stars awaken, bright and clear.
Moonlight dances on the bay,
Night enfolds the end of day.

Shadows stretch and gently sway,
In the quiet, dreams find play.
Colors blend, a soft embrace,
Nature's lullaby finds its place.

The horizon's edge begins to fade,
With every breath, the stillness made.
Whispers travel on the breeze,
Promising peace beneath the trees.

The world adorned in silver light,
Cradled in the arms of night.
Crickets serenade, their song,
In this moment, we belong.

Shimmering night, a fleeting sight,
Moments caught in pure delight.
In every star, a tale to tell,
In the darkness, all is well.

Ethereal Glaciers

Beneath the skies, a frozen sea,
Ethereal glaciers wild and free.
Crystal peaks in purest white,
Whispers of the heart's delight.

A stillness reigns in twilight's glow,
Where time stands still, and breezes flow.
The world in peace, a serene stage,
Nature's beauty, age to age.

Reflections dance on icy glass,
Ancient secrets in layers pass.
The air so crisp, a breath divine,
In every flake, a perfect sign.

Nature's power, quiet yet grand,
Holding stories of this land.
Listen close, hear the ice breathe,
In this moment, we believe.

Ethereal wonders in the light,
Glaciers sparkle, pure and bright.
In their silence, wisdom shared,
In this realm, all hearts are bared.

Polished Nebulae

In cosmos vast, where wonders lie,
Polished nebulae catch the eye.
Colors weave through dark's embrace,
Secrets held in stellar space.

Whirling clouds of dust and light,
Crafting visions, bold and bright.
In their dance, the stars are born,
From the chaos, new worlds worn.

Galaxies spin in graceful arcs,
In whispered tales, they leave their marks.
Nebulous forms, both dream and real,
Awakening the heart to feel.

Radiant hues paint the night,
Crafting magic, pure delight.
In silence, knowledge flows like streams,
Lighting paths to cosmic dreams.

Through polished depths, we gaze in sight,
Chasing echoes of the light.
In every swirl, our hearts entwined,
In the universe, we seek and find.

Cold Radiance

In shadows cast by winter's breath,
Cold radiance speaks of silent death.
Crystal frost on branches glows,
A beauty born where cold wind flows.

The world is lost in icy dreams,
Where moonlight shimmers, softly gleams.
Every flake, a story spun,
In this stillness, we are one.

A hush envelops, whispers call,
In the quiet, we feel it all.
Nature's breath in icy air,
Reminds us of our simple care.

The chill wraps 'round with tender grace,
Comfort found in nature's face.
In frozen realms, the heart ignites,
Embracing warmth in coldest nights.

Cold radiance, a fleeting glow,
Encapsulating everything we know.
In every chill, a warmth resides,
In every heart, the love abides.

Crystalline Whispers

In the hush of dawn's embrace,
Sparkling light takes its place.
Gentle murmurs fill the air,
Nature's secrets, softly rare.

Each flake dances, pure and bright,
Whispers of a winter night.
Silent tales in silver threads,
On the ground, soft dreams are spread.

Branches bow beneath the weight,
Crystalline, they fascinate.
Echoes of a world asleep,
In this calm, the spirits leap.

Beneath the sky's vast expanse,
Frozen wonders weave and dance.
A tapestry of frost and gleam,
Whispers weave a fleeting dream.

Lost in moments, time does freeze,
Captured in the winter's tease.
Crystalline, the world is spun,
Whispers chill, yet warmth has spun.

Vast Chills

Through the woods where shadows creep,
Vast chills come as day does sleep.
Frosty gusts in silence sweep,
Nature holds its breath, so deep.

Icicle tears from branches hang,
In the night, the soft winds sang.
Echoing in the moon's white glow,
Whispers of the cold below.

Mountains draped in purest white,
Guardians of the starry night.
Frozen rivers, still as glass,
Reflecting dreams that come to pass.

Pine trees wear their icy crowns,
Vast chills cloak the sleeping towns.
Every breath, a whisper's trace,
In this wild, untouched space.

Steps crunch softly, breaking peace,
In this frost, the troubles cease.
Nature's grace in every flake,
Vast chills weave the paths we take.

Frosted Orbs

Gathered round, the frosted orbs,
Shimmering with timeless lore.
Each one tells a tale untold,
Whispers of the world so cold.

On the branches, crystals gleam,
Frosted spheres as if in dream.
Captured light in winter's hold,
Radiance in hues of gold.

Underneath the starry dome,
Frosted orbs, they call us home.
Softly glowing, night unwinds,
Magic lingers, love entwines.

Quiet moments, time stands still,
Frosted visions, hearts to fill.
Luminous against the night,
Orbs of wonder, pure delight.

Through the dark, they guide the way,
Frosted orbs shall gently sway.
In their glow, the world transcends,
Fantasy, where winter bends.

Celestial Winterscape

Underneath a silver sky,
Celestial winterscape up high.
Clouds like feathers, soft and white,
Blanket the earth, a tranquil sight.

Stars emerge, in splendor gleam,
Filling hearts with a quiet dream.
Mountains rise, majestic, bold,
Veiled in white, a sight to hold.

Crystalline rivers carve the land,
Whispering journeys, soft and grand.
While the night wraps, warm and deep,
Secrets linger where shadows creep.

Snowflakes fall like whispered tales,
Dancing lightly on the gales.
Every flake unique and rare,
Celestial wonders fill the air.

Through this landscape, calm prevails,
In the night, serenity sails.
Celestial dreams in every breath,
Whispers of love, life, and death.

Celestial Stillness

Stars whisper softly, in the night,
Moonlight dances, casting gentle light.
The world holds its breath, so serene,
In the glow of dreams, a silent scene.

Winds caress the trees, a hushed tone,
Nature embraces, never alone.
Crickets serenade, a quiet song,
In this stillness, we all belong.

Clouds drift slowly, far above,
Drifting gently, like a dove.
Time stands still, a moment's grace,
In celestial stillness, we find our place.

As night unfolds, mysteries unfold,
Stories whispered, secrets told.
Beneath the stars, wonder awaits,
In the calm, the heart elevates.

Tomorrow's dawn will break the trance,
But for now, we embrace the dance.
In the still of night, we're free,
Bound by the cosmos, you and me.

Luminosity of Ice

Glacial crystals shine so bright,
Reflecting whispers of pure light.
Each facet catches winter's glow,
In a world untouched by woe.

Frozen rivers, silent streams,
Nature's canvas of frosty dreams.
Every flake a silent kiss,
In the chill, we find our bliss.

Icicles hanging from the eaves,
Nature weaves with silver leaves.
In a tapestry, so divine,
Luminosity of ice aligns.

Underneath the winter's stare,
Frosted branches sway in air.
A symphony of crystal chimes,
Echoing through frozen climes.

As the sun begins to rise,
Colors burst, a sweet surprise.
Yet still, in shadows cool and nice,
We cherish nature's soft device.

Midnight Frost

In the hush of midnight's breath,
Frost blankets earth, a dance with death.
Whispers echo, soft as a sigh,
Under a star-speckled sky.

Every blade of grass enshrined,
In icy shards, beauty aligned.
Moonlight glimmers on the ground,
In stark serenity, peace is found.

Trees adorned with crystal lace,
Nature's beauty, a timeless grace.
In the stillness, hearts convene,
To marvel at the winter scene.

As shadows stretch and daylight flees,
Chill hangs heavy in the trees.
Yet in this frozen, quiet time,
Life's heartbeat echoes, slow yet prime.

Midnight frost, a gift endowed,
Nature's silence, deep and proud.
In winter's grasp, we find the space,
To bask in the night's soft embrace.

Ethereal Chill

A whisper of wind, cold yet sweet,
Nature's breath, a rhythmic beat.
Clouds drift softly, drifting dreams,
In the night's embrace, silence gleams.

Stars twinkle like forgotten tales,
Guiding through the frostbitten trails.
Each moment fleeting, yet it stays,
In ethereal chill, where magic plays.

Beneath the moon's soft gaze, we tread,
Through silver landscapes, lightly fed.
Every breath a cloud of mist,
In the cold embrace, we coexist.

Journeying through the starry night,
Where echoes of laughter take flight.
A blanket of stars, a quilt so vast,
In the chill of the night, shadows cast.

When dawn arrives to break the spell,
We'll carry memories, to keep and tell.
Yet in the chill of night so fine,
We find our solace, and we shine.

Aeons of Chill

In the whisper of the night,
Frost creeps across the ground.
Frozen breath steals the light,
In silence, peace is found.

Old trees shiver in the breeze,
Crystals glint, a silver sheen.
Nature's song, a soft freeze,
Echoes through the tranquil scene.

Stars blink in the ocean of dark,
Casting shadows, pale and bright.
Each flake falls, a quiet spark,
A dance in the frosty night.

Memory drifts, like smoke's trace,
Within a realm of icy dreams.
Time has halted in this space,
Whispers flow in moonlit streams.

In the end, what remains clear,
The chill is not just of air.
It lingers in hearts held dear,
A timeless bond, beyond compare.

Twilight's Icy Embrace

As twilight falls, the chill awakes,
Softly wrapped in frost's embrace.
Bare branches sway, the silence quakes,
Underneath a silver grace.

Shadows stretch, they weave and glide,
Night's canvas painted deep and wide.
Cold winds whisper, they won't hide,
Secrets in the snow abide.

Moonlight dances on the stream,
Casting dreams in pools of night.
Each reflection, a quiet beam,
A moment held, pure and bright.

Crystals form on windowsills,
Nature's art in frozen time.
Every breath a rush, it chills,
While stars above in rhythm chime.

Hearts may feel this winter's bite,
Yet warmth resides in shared glance.
In the cold, love shines so bright,
Encased in time's unyielding dance.

Frozen Echoes

In the stillness, whispers rise,
Echoes of a frozen past.
Chilled by time, a soft sigh,
Lost in depths that hold it fast.

Footprints left in crystal snow,
Tell of journeys, wild and free.
Where did all the wanderers go?
Embraced by winter's mystery.

Frosty breath upon the glass,
Misty shapes that fade away.
Moments frozen, never pass,
In the twilight, shadows play.

Deep within the icy heart,
Lies a warmth that never wanes.
Life and death, they intertwine,
In this world that ever reigns.

Even in the coldest nights,
Hope is born, a fragile light.
Silent dreams take to their flights,
Forever held in snowy sights.

Stelliferous Glace

Underneath the starry shroud,
Frozen dreams begin their flight.
Whispers soft, yet oh so loud,
In the depths of endless night.

Shimmering on the snow so bright,
Every twinkle holds a tale.
Once in darkness, now the light,
Guiding souls through winter's veil.

Layers thick of crystal clear,
Veil the earth in glistening dress.
Each moment felt, each whispered near,
Draws us close in nature's caress.

Echoes linger in the still,
Every heartbeat, every pulse.
Even in the cold, the thrill,
Links our spirits, intertwines, rolls.

Stars above, a silver lace,
In the quiet, dreams awake.
Life and love, a warm embrace,
In the chill, our hearts won't break.

Translucent Stardust

In the quiet night sky, they gleam,
Whispers of wishes, a celestial dream.
Dancing like fireflies, they softly sway,
Translucent stardust, guiding our way.

Fleeting moments, time slips by,
A melody of silence, under a sigh.
Each spark a memory, vibrant and bright,
Holding the secrets of the endless night.

They twinkle with hope, a shimmering tune,
Painting our hearts beneath the moon.
In the tapestry of cosmos, they delight,
Translucent stardust, our hearts ignite.

Floating through dreams, a gentle embrace,
In their glow, we find our place.
Carried on winds of soft twilight,
Translucent stardust, a blissful sight.

So when you gaze up, remember to see,
The whisper of dreams, as vast as the sea.
Each twinkle a promise, every light a kiss,
Translucent stardust, a glimpse of bliss.

Stellar Breezes

In the cosmic ocean, breezes swirl,
Carrying tales of the universe's pearl.
Soft like a feather, they drift through the night,
Stellar breezes, igniting our light.

They whisper of secrets, of ages gone by,
Crossing the valleys of starlit sky.
A dance of the cosmos, tender and free,
Stellar breezes, calling to me.

Through nebulae bright, they twist and twine,
Drawing us closer, in their divine line.
Breath of the stars, a gentle caress,
Stellar breezes, in cosmic finesse.

With every pulse, they carry our dreams,
In their embrace, nothing's as it seems.
Floating on currents, vast and serene,
Stellar breezes, where we have been.

So let them guide you, through dark and light,
A voyage of wonder, in the soft night.
With every sigh, feel the universe tease,
Stellar breezes, our hearts at ease.

Crystalline Infinity

Reflection of beauty, a prism of light,
Crystalline infinity, sparkling bright.
Each facet a story, a moment in time,
Shimmering visions, so pure and sublime.

In the heart of the cosmos, they softly call,
Images woven through the vast sprawl.
A dance of dimensions, ever so grand,
Crystalline infinity, woven by hand.

Echoes of stardust, a delicate thread,
Linking the cosmos, where wonders are spread.
In silent reflections, we find our peace,
Crystalline infinity, where all troubles cease.

Flowing like rivers, they shimmer and shine,
In the depths of the universe, a treasure divine.
With each fleeting glance, feel the universe sing,
Crystalline infinity, a beautiful thing.

So pause and behold, this shimmering sea,
In its timeless span, find your heart's decree.
Through the prism of dreams, let your spirit soar,
Crystalline infinity, forevermore.

Lunar Frost

Under the gaze of the silver moon,
Whispers of frost sing a tender tune.
Delicate crystals, a shimmering lace,
Lunar frost dances, a magical grace.

In the chill of the night, they weave and twine,
Transforming the world into splendor divine.
A gentle embrace, soft and so pure,
Lunar frost, mysterious allure.

Each step upon earth, a crunching delight,
Echoing magic beneath the starlight.
Nature's embrace in the still of the night,
Lunar frost glistens, a wondrous sight.

With every shimmer, dreams take their flight,
In the breath of the cold, heart takes its height.
A tapestry woven of night's gentle breath,
Lunar frost whispers of life and death.

So linger and dream 'neath the moon's soft glow,
Let the lunar frost guide where you go.
In the silence of night, feel the frost's gentle bite,
Lunar frost cradles the world in its light.

Celestial Icebound

In the depths where silence dwells,
Stars are frozen, secrets swell.
Crystals spark in moonlit glow,
Whispers of the night winds blow.

Frozen dreams in silver light,
Chasing shadows, taking flight.
A realm where time stands still,
Nature's heart, a quiet thrill.

Galaxies weave through icy streams,
Wrapped in soft, celestial dreams.
Each twinkle tells a frozen tale,
Echoes soft as winter's veil.

Through the void, the silence sings,
Glistening like ethereal wings.
This dance of frost, a cosmic trance,
In the stillness, we entranced.

Celestial realms, so vast, so deep,
Where secrets lie in frozen keep.
Among the stars, our spirits soar,
In the icebound night, we explore.

Shards of Night

In the void, where shadows creep,
Stars like shards in silence peep.
Mystic tales of darkness spun,
Whispers soft as daylight's done.

Each shard a glimmer, rare and bright,
Dancing softly in the night.
Fragments of forgotten dreams,
Caught in silver, moonlit beams.

Cracks of light through darkened skies,
Echoes of the night's reprise.
Glittering phantoms spin and weave,
In their embrace, we believe.

Sculpted by time, they drift and play,
Guiding us through night's ballet.
Glistening paths where wishes climb,
Shards of night, eternal rhyme.

Here in darkness, secrets bide,
Underneath the starlit tide.
In the shadows, dreams ignite,
In the beauty of the night.

Glistening Nebulae

In the fabric of twilight's hue,
Nebulae dance, vibrant and new.
Colors swirl in cosmic embrace,
Painting the void with grace.

Glistening clouds of gas and light,
Whispering tales of the night.
Creation sings from every seam,
In the heart of a stellar dream.

Clouds ablaze with colors bright,
Cradle stars in silken night.
Each pulse a heartbeat, drawing near,
Nebulae's anthem, crystal clear.

Amongst the swirls of time and space,
Lies the universe's warm embrace.
Every glow a story told,
In the cosmos, bright and bold.

Nebulae gleam with the tales of yore,
Fried and churned like celestial lore.
Journey with me through the vast unknown,
In starlit beauty, we have grown.

Subzero Brilliance

In the chill of winter's breath,
Stars are born where light meets death.
Icicles hang like frozen sighs,
Underneath the darkened skies.

Brilliance shines through layers cold,
In the silence, wonders unfold.
Frosted air and glimmering sheen,
Nature's art, a tranquil scene.

Subzero realms, untouched, pristine,
Glistening bright, a radiant sheen.
Stillness holds a world so grand,
In every crystal, a dream is planned.

Brush of ice on hopes aglow,
Cold embraces, beauty flows.
Refracted light through prism's frame,
Subzero brilliance fuels the flame.

Here in frost, the universe sighs,
In splendor bright, the spirit flies.
Every flake a memory's dance,
In the cold, we find romance.

Glacial Gleams

In the still of night, they glow,
A silvery dance, a silent show.
Whispers of ice in the gentle breeze,
Crystals shimmer with such ease.

Frozen lakes and moonlit skies,
Nature's art, a pure surprise.
Each breath a mist, each step a dream,
In the glow of glacial gleam.

The world dressed in a pale white veil,
Soft shadows weave, a ghostly trail.
Wonders awaken in the night's embrace,
Frosty fingers trace nature's face.

A chorus of stars in the vast above,
Each twinkle a note, a hymn of love.
Time stands still in this frozen land,
Where beauty waits, silent and grand.

In the heart of winter's chill,
Every moment, a magic thrill.
Glacial whispers call the wise,
In the night of glacial skies.

Cosmic Frost

Upon the dawn, a blanket wide,
Crystals wake, no place to hide.
Stars on earth, they softly shine,
In the grasp of winter's vine.

Galaxies twirl in a frozen dance,
Each flake sparkles in a trance.
A cosmic hush blankets the globe,
In this icy, ethereal robe.

Night unfolds with its frosty breath,
Where silence reigns, and echoes rest.
Nebulas form in the chilly air,
An astral glow, beyond compare.

Stardust falls, a soft embrace,
Each particle finds a sacred place.
Together they weave, a gleaming frost,
In this boundless space, all else is lost.

Look to the skies, let wonder flow,
As cosmic frost begins to grow.
Eternity whispers through the ice,
In worlds unknown, so precise.

Radiant Chills

Awakening dawn with a frosted hue,
Nature's breath whispers, soft and true.
A canvas of white, serene and vast,
Moments of beauty, forever cast.

Radiant chills across the glen,
Gentle edges where time begins.
Layers of snow, like whispered tales,
Painting silence as winter prevails.

Each step crunches, a crisp embrace,
Textures hidden in winter's grace.
Colors fade in the fading light,
Radiance calls through the cold night.

Embers glisten, lost in dreams,
Where soft murmurs dance in gleams.
The world wrapped tight in a chilly lace,
Every heartbeat finds its place.

With winter's charm, the season sways,
In radiant chills, we seek new ways.
Every breath lingers, soft and bright,
As day surrenders to the night.

Stellar Winter

Stars collide in a canvas of night,
Winter's chill brings forth pure light.
Each sparkle dances across the snow,
Where dreams take flight, and whispers flow.

A tapestry of frost, woven fine,
Cosmic patterns that intertwine.
Stellar secrets in the cold embrace,
Each glimmer carries a timeless trace.

Mountains clad in a glistening shroud,
Echoes of silence, proud and loud.
Beneath the heavens, a story's spun,
In the heart of winter, where we run.

Crystals form on the branches high,
A shimmering symphony in the sky.
Every moment holds a wondrous thrill,
In the magic of the winter's will.

So take a breath, let wonder reign,
In stellar winter, joy and pain.
Nature's promise under the stars,
A cosmic dance that heals our scars.

Icy Celestial Dance

Beneath the stars that brightly gleam,
A waltz of frost begins to dream.
The moonlight whispers through the trees,
While winter's breath sways gently, free.

The air is crisp, the night so still,
Each flake a dancer, poised, surreal.
They spiral down in twinkling grace,
Embraced by shadows, they find their place.

The cosmos spins in silent awe,
As nature's magic leaves us raw.
A symphony of cold and light,
In this enchanted, starry night.

Time slips away in the frosted air,
As if the world has paused, laid bare.
Each sparkling speck a fleeting chance,
In this icy, celestial dance.

Beneath the sky, our hearts draw near,
Tangled closely in frosty cheer.
Together we twirl, lost in a trance,
Forever held in winter's glance.

Whispers in the Frost

In twilight hues where shadows creep,
The frost awakens from its sleep.
It blankets earth in sparkling white,
And whispers secrets of the night.

Every breath is a frosted sigh,
As silence blankets, soft and sigh.
The trees stand tall, adorned with lace,
Crystals that catch the moon's embrace.

Footfalls crunch on frozen ground,
In the stillness, truths abound.
The winter's chill, a gentle throat,
Painting a tale, barely wrote.

Beneath the stars, the world lies still,
Each moment captured by winter's will.
As whispers weave through the cold air,
Frosty secrets linger there.

In the quiet night's embrace we find,
Nature's whispers, tender, kind.
A bond forged in the freeze of time,
With every frost, a silent rhyme.

Glittering Nightfall

As daylight fades to twilight's glow,
The stars emerge, one by one, slow.
The velvet sky begins to twinkle,
In night's embrace, dreams start to sprinkle.

Each star a gem, the heavens gleam,
Awakening the night's sweet dream.
The moon rises, a haunting sight,
Casting shadows in soft moonlight.

In the silence, secrets soar,
Every glimmer, a crafted lore.
As constellations begin to trace,
The stories woven in endless space.

Soft whispers echo through the dark,
As night unveils its timeless spark.
The universe in a gentle sway,
With glittering grace, leads us away.

To dance among the stars so bright,
In the beauty of the endless night.
We roam through dreams, free as air,
In the glittering embrace we share.

Cosmic Chill

The cosmos hums a chilling tune,
As night descends beneath the moon.
Stars flicker in the vast expanse,
Inviting hearts to take a chance.

The cold air wraps around so tight,
Cocooning dreams within its light.
Each breath we take is crisp and clear,
In this quiet realm, we draw near.

The galaxies spin, a twinkling ballet,
In the embrace of the Milky Way.
Infinite wonders within our reach,
The cosmos whispers, silence to teach.

In the blackness, beauty shines bright,
As we lose ourselves in the cosmic night.
Every moment a fleeting thrill,
Caught in the grasp of cosmic chill.

Stars ignite with a fiery grace,
Guiding our hearts through time and space.
Embraced by night, our spirits fly,
In the chill of the vast, endless sky.

Chilling Nebulae

In the dark expanse where shadows dance,
Colors swirl in a silent trance.
Whispers of stars born in the night,
Cradled gently in cosmic light.

Frosty winds move through the void,
Echoes of dreams yet unvoiced.
Nebulous forms sprawled wide and far,
Guided softly by a distant star.

Veils of mist, a clinging shroud,
They drift through the heavens, soft yet proud.
A tapestry woven from time and space,
In chilling beauty, they find their place.

Celestial wonders flicker and glow,
Stories buried in a cosmic flow.
Each breath of twilight a silent sigh,
As nebulae cradle the secrets of sky.

Unveiling mysteries, unfurling fate,
In the stillness where silence waits.
Chilling nebulae, vast and grand,
Remnants of worlds in a timeless land.

Astral Glaciers

Glistening blue in a void so deep,
Ancient echoes, secrets they keep.
Winding slowly through the black,
Astral glaciers on their timeless track.

Frost-kissed edges twinkling bright,
Interstellar wonders capturing light.
Their icy trails tell tales of yore,
Of cosmic shores and celestial lore.

Majestic stillness, a frozen roar,
Slicing space with a spectral score.
In this realm where time stands still,
Glaciers of stars, beauty they instill.

Drifting slowly, surreal and pure,
Nature's art, an ever-living lure.
Echos of light that time forgot,
In astral glaciers, peace is caught.

Crystals shimmering against the night,
Each glimmer holds a spark of light.
Within their grasp, the universe sighs,
As astral glaciers roam the skies.

Radiant Winter Skies

Golden hues paint the twilight's edge,
As day bids farewell from its ledge.
Snowflakes sparkle in the fading light,
Embracing the chill of the coming night.

Stars awaken with a gentle gleam,
In winter's embrace, they softly beam.
A canvas hung in the cosmos' might,
Radiant colors dancing in flight.

Whispers of frost weave through the air,
Fleeting moments, beyond compare.
The heavens hum a celestial song,
In winter's arms where dreams belong.

Crystalline visions, a stunning sight,
Under the glow of the silver light.
Tranquil beauty, so profound,
Radiant skies where peace is found.

In the night's embrace, we find our glow,
As winter weaves her magic show.
Hearts alight with celestial spark,
In radiant skies, we leave our mark.

Stellar Fragments in Ice

Scattered shards of a fallen star,
Frozen whispers from places far.
Crystalline edges in twilight's breath,
Remnants of light, a dance with death.

Each fragment tells a story old,
Of cosmic battles and worlds untold.
Captured brilliance in silence resides,
In icy prisons where wonder hides.

Galactic echoes in shivering hues,
Reflecting dreams that night renews.
In the wilderness where silence breathes,
Stellar fragments weave their weaves.

Time suspends in a frosty grasp,
As mysteries linger and softly clasp.
Born from the void, embraced by night,
In the cold recoil, they find their light.

Fleeting moments of beauty so rare,
In the heart of ice, they bloom with flair.
Echoes of starlight, forever precise,
In the magic of stellar fragments in ice.

Frigid Dreams

In the stillness of night, cold winds sigh,
Whispers of frost gently pass by.
Beneath a blanket of shimmering white,
Frigid dreams dance in soft moonlight.

Snowflakes twirl in a silent ballet,
Carving memories where shadows play.
Each breath of winter, a crystal clear phase,
In this enchanted, frozen haze.

The world transformed, a serene display,
Nature's canvas in shades of gray.
Time stands still, as if to say,
In frigid realms, we dream away.

Stars emerge in the night's embrace,
Light bursts forth, a celestial trace.
Guiding wanderers through icy streams,
Caressing thoughts with frigid dreams.

Awakening to the dawn's soft glow,
The night retreats, the sun's warm flow.
Yet in our hearts, we'll always know,
Frigid dreams linger, like fresh-fallen snow.

Sparkling Silence

Beneath a vast and starry dome,
The world is hushed, and feels like home.
Crystals shimmer on branches bare,
In sparkling silence, we find our lair.

Echoes fade in the quiet air,
Snow blankets all without a care.
Footsteps muffled, a gentle tread,
In this stillness, our hearts are fed.

Every breath a cloud, soft and light,
Time drifts slowly in the moonlight.
A tapestry woven with frost and grace,
In sparkling silence, we find our place.

The night whispers secrets, old and wise,
Unraveling stories under dark skies.
In this calm, we dare to dream,
Where sparkling silence reigns supreme.

When the dawn breaks, the stillness fades,
Yet echoes of peace the day cascades.
In our souls, the memory gleams,
Of nights spent in sparkling dreams.

Astral Ice

Underneath a sky so vast and deep,
A realm of wonders, where starlight weeps.
Astral ice glimmers, a cosmic stage,
Dancing suns trapped in a frozen cage.

Nebulas swirl with colors bright,
Painting the darkness, igniting the night.
Luminous trails weave through the air,
A ballet of orbs, beyond compare.

Whispers of galaxies echo near,
Carried on winds we long to hear.
Celestial bodies in twinkling grace,
In astral ice, we carve our place.

Supernovas burst with a vibrant sigh,
Transforming darkness, lighting the sky.
Celebrations of worlds, distant yet close,
In our dreams, it's the cosmos we chose.

As dawn approaches, the stars retreat,
Yet in our hearts, their rhythm beats.
Astral ice lingers as we glance,
At the universe's endless dance.

Winter's Embrace

Wrapped in the arms of winter's chill,
Nature whispers; the world feels still.
Frost-kissed trees stand tall and wide,
In winter's embrace, we choose to hide.

Beneath the blanket of soft, white snow,
Dreams come alive, and feelings flow.
The air is crisp, each breath divine,
In this embrace, our hopes align.

Echoes of laughter fill the air,
Sleds racing down the slopes, a carefree affair.
Warmth of fires crackling bright,
Our hearts glow in the long, cold night.

Snowflakes dance with a gentle grace,
Each unique pattern a soft embrace.
In this season, time moves slow,
Winter's embrace teaches us to grow.

As days grow short and nights expand,
We hold our loved ones, hand in hand.
Wrapped in a hope that winter brings,
In winter's embrace, our spirit sings.

Night's Frosted Serenade

Moonlight's kiss on frozen ground,
Whispers soft, a night profound.
Stars above in velvet black,
Nature sings, no light to lack.

Trees adorned in silver lace,
Stillness wrapped, a tender grace.
Echoes dance through icy air,
Lullabies, a dream laid bare.

Crisp the breath, a world asleep,
Dreams adrift in shadows deep.
Each soft flake, a note in tune,
Harmony beneath the moon.

Frosty breath of winter's hand,
Cocooned in a crystal band.
Earth and sky, a mirrored state,
Weathered hearts, no room for hate.

In the night, when silence reigns,
Magic whispers through the pines.
Frosted serenade unfolds,
In the dark, the night beholds.

Chilling Cosmic Echoes

In the void where silence sways,
Chilling echoes mark the days.
Colder than a distant star,
Whispers travel, near and far.

Galaxy's embrace, so wide,
Drifting worlds in stellar tide.
Cold caress on cosmic skin,
Secrets locked, where dreams begin.

Frigid trails of ancient light,
Kiss the dark, dissolve the night.
Time and space in frozen flow,
Eternal dance, a silent show.

In the dark, a haunting sound,
Chilling echoes all around.
Mysteries in shadows crawl,
Cosmic whispers heed their call.

Stardust weaves a fragile thread,
In the stillness, truths are spread.
Chilling cosmos, dreams align,
Lost in space, forever blind.

Glacial Light

A shimmer on the crystal sea,
Glacial light, a sight to be.
Underneath the azure sky,
Breath of winter, soft and shy.

Icebergs drift with quiet might,
Casting shadows, purest white.
Nature's mirror, bold yet meek,
Whispers of the ice they speak.

Radiance in a frozen land,
Where the frost and dreams expand.
In the chill, there lies a glow,
A testament to life below.

Glacial light, a fleeting spark,
Illuminates the muted dark.
Time stands still in nature's gaze,
Forever lost in icy haze.

Waves that dance with frosty breath,
Carving paths of life and death.
In this realm, serenity,
A tranquil pulse, eternity.

Shimmers of the Cosmos

Nebulae in twilight's grip,
Shimmers of the cosmos slip.
Colors blend with twilight rays,
In the dark, the stardust plays.

Veils of night, a rich embrace,
Every shimmer finds its place.
Galactic dreams suspended high,
Breath of wonder, never shy.

In the silence, secrets weave,
All around, the cosmos breathe.
Stars align in rhythmic dance,
Each a spark of fate's romance.

Eons whisper through the light,
Shimmers gleam, a guiding sight.
Through the vast, an endless song,
In the cosmos, we belong.

Twinkling hopes in the night sky,
Shimmers rise and never die.
Boundless realms where dreams ignite,
In the dark, we find our light.

The Chill of Infinity

In the void where silence dwells,
Stars ignite in whispered spells.
Time unfolds, a frozen breath,
Warming cold, yet hinting death.

Nebulas swirl in twilight blue,
Eons pass, yet still feel new.
Galaxies dance in endless flight,
A cosmic waltz of day and night.

Whispers echo, shadows roam,
The chill wraps around like foam.
Every heartbeat breaks the dark,
Infinite dreams, a frozen spark.

Endless depths, vast and deep,
Where secrets of the cosmos sleep.
Stars collide, their stories shared,
In this chill, we are ensnared.

Light flickers from the great unknown,
In chilling folds of void we've grown.
A tapestry of night unfurled,
The chill of infinity, our world.

Cosmic Snowflakes

Falling softly from the skies,
Each snowflake whispers, gently flies.
Crafted from starry dust and dreams,
Floating through cosmic beams.

They swirl in silence, pure and bright,
Painting the canvas of the night.
Each a story, unique and rare,
Merkaba dreams in the quiet air.

Galaxies sprinkle and take their flight,
Across the cosmos, an endless sight.
Wrapped in stillness, without a sound,
The beauty of space, in silence found.

Waltzing wonders, gleaming white,
Transforming darkness, gifting light.
Cosmic snowflakes, a celestial art,
Weaving together worlds apart.

As they descend, we stand in awe,
Nature's magic, a perfect law.
Softly landing, a wonder's grace,
Cosmic snowflakes, time and space.

Shivering Galaxies

In the dark, they twist and twine,
Shimmering under cosmic sign.
Breathtaking tales, in colors gleam,
Shivering galaxies, lost in dream.

Waves of light stretch and bend,
Through the cold, they twist and mend.
Celestial bodies in a fray,
Dancing softly, night and day.

Stars ignite with fervent flare,
Breath of cosmos, frozen air.
Vortex rumbles, silence breaks,
In the depths, creation wakes.

Infinite realms, a wondrous sight,
Within the dark, they shine so bright.
Whispers of time, shivering threads,
Galaxies stir where silence treads.

Life emerges in frozen light,
In every shiver, pure delight.
Cosmic ballet, without a sound,
Shivering galaxies, beauty found.

Light in the Frost

In the stillness, a glimmer shines,
Frosted whispers, in perfect lines.
Hope ignites in the crystal chill,
A beacon glows, a warming thrill.

Through winter's grasp, the light breaks free,
Painting shadows on the tree.
Each breath mist forms a spell,
In the heart, a gentle swell.

Dancing softly on sleet and ice,
Illuminating paths, so precise.
This chilly world, yet warmed by grace,
A light that warms every space.

Stars like diamonds in frosty skies,
Guide us home with sparkling eyes.
Through the dark, the journey goes,
Light in the frost, our comfort grows.

And as the dawn begins to rise,
Frosted crystals meet the skies.
In every glimmer, find your way,
Light in the frost, a brand new day.

Silent Celestials

Stars whisper secrets, soft and low,
In the night sky's gentle glow.
Moonlight dances on tranquil lakes,
While the world dreams, slumber wakes.

Time pauses, wrapped in velvet night,
As constellations weave their light.
Galaxies swirl in endless space,
Silent dance, a cosmic grace.

Wonders lie beyond the veil,
In each twinkling, an ancient tale.
Hearts lift with the cosmic tide,
In the silence, dreams abide.

Whispers of worlds long gone,
In the stillness, they live on.
A vast expanse, a canvas deep,
Where memories of starlight sleep.

Eternal night, yet warm and bright,
Silent celestials, pure delight.
In their glow, we find our place,
Boundless dreams in time and space.

Frostbitten Horizons

Dawn breaks, a canvas of icy blue,
Where whispers of winter's breath ensue.
Frosty tendrils cling to the trees,
Glittering diamonds in the breeze.

A chill resonates in the morning air,
Silence reigns, nature does care.
Footprints trace paths on powdered snow,
Each step tells tales of where we go.

Mountains rise, draped in white,
Guardians of the frosted night.
Sunlight dances, rays glisten bright,
Painting horizons in pure delight.

The world holds its breath, still and clear,
In this frozen realm, we hold dear.
Each breath a fog, a moment to keep,
In the heart of winter, secrets sleep.

Frostbitten dreams in the frosty glow,
Where silenced echoes gently flow.
In every flake, a promise made,
Underneath, life's fabric laid.

Cryptic Luminosity

Glimmers flicker through veils of black,
Shadows dance, there's no turning back.
A light that beckons, yet haunts the soul,
Mysteries swirl, beyond control.

Silent whispers in the dark arise,
Hints of truth in the midnight skies.
They draw the curious, they call the brave,
To unravel secrets, the dark world gave.

A shimmer on water reflects the stars,
Concert of brilliance behind locked bars.
Every twinkle, a riddle profound,
In their enigma, answers abound.

Yet beware the allure of the glow,
For shadows lurk where few dare go.
Each path leads to realms unknown,
In cryptic luminosity, we're never alone.

Illuminate the questions that lay in wait,
With whispers of light, we navigate fate.
To find the meaning in shadows cast,
In the dance of the luminous, we breathe our last.

Subzero Wonders

Below the frost, the earth lies still,
A world of wonders, nature's will.
Icicles hang like glassy spears,
Crafted truths from frozen years.

Amidst the chill, life finds its way,
In the quiet hours of the day.
Whispers of life in a winter's vale,
Stories woven in each icy trail.

Crystals form on every leaf,
Nature's art, beyond belief.
In the heart of frost, beauty blooms,
Amid the cold, the spirit resumes.

Stars shine bright in the azure dome,
Subzero wonders, their eternal home.
A tapestry woven with threads of gold,
Where frost and fire together unfold.

In every breath, a spark ignites,
In the silence, a chorus of lights.
Subzero wonders, forever last,
A dance of seasons, futures cast.

Sparkling in Stillness

In the hush of twilight's grace,
Stars begin their gentle chase.
Whispers dance on evening's breath,
Moments linger, free from death.

Crickets sing a serenade,
Silhouettes in shadows made.
Moonlight weaves through velvet night,
Crafting dreams in silver light.

Ripples form on tranquil streams,
Reflecting softly woven dreams.
A canvas painted by the night,
Where heartbeats swell and take their flight.

Branches sway with secrets deep,
Nature's lullaby to keep.
In stillness, life begins to flow,
A tranquil dance, a gentle show.

Breathe in peace, let worries fade,
In this stillness, we have stayed.
Every spark a whispered prayer,
In the night, all burdens rare.

Winter's Celestial Veil

Snowflakes drift from skies so gray,
Wrapping the world in bright array.
Silent nights and frosty air,
Nature's calm, a dream to share.

Underneath the starlit dome,
For a while, the world feels home.
Whispers through the frosted trees,
Echo softly on the breeze.

Icicles hang like crystal spears,
Holding time, and stifled fears.
In their glow, a tranquil scene,
Winter's magic, pure and keen.

Footprints mark the way we tread,
Each a story, softly said.
In this hush, we seek to find,
The warmth that glows within the mind.

As dawn breaks with a golden hue,
Winter's veil bids us adieu.
Yet in hearts, its chill remains,
A gentle touch of soft refrains.

Shimmering Eternity

In the depths of endless time,
Moments glisten, subtle rhyme.
Whispers echo in the void,
Every heartbeat, sweetly buoyed.

Stars above begin to twinkle,
Memories fade and softly crinkle.
Time unfolds its layered song,
In its arms, where we belong.

Glimmers of a life well lived,
All the secrets that we'd give.
Chasing shadows, weaving light,
Eternity embraces night.

Each breath shared, a thread of gold,
Stories waiting to be told.
Shimmering like waters deep,
In the silence, dreams will leap.

Hold this moment, feel it swell,
In this realm where spirits dwell.
Together in the cosmic dance,
Finding peace, love's sweet romance.

Radiance of the Abyss

In the depth of darkest seas,
Lies a glow that softly frees.
Whispers of the ancient tides,
Secrets where the silence hides.

Coral dreams and shadowed light,
Dancing in the velvet night.
Every ripple tells a tale,
Of the strength that won't grow pale.

Creatures move in harmony,
Embracing all that's meant to be.
In the shadows, lives entwine,
Love and hope in every line.

Echoes of forgotten sun,
In the deep, we come undone.
Finding wisdom in each wave,
A reminder to be brave.

Here, beneath the endless waves,
Life's bright pulse, the heart it saves.
Radiance in every breath,
In the abyss, we conquer death.

Icy Echoes

In the stillness, whispers sing,
Frozen wonders softly cling.
Echoes dance on frozen streams,
Crafting melodies from dreams.

Snowflakes twirl in gentle flight,
Chasing shadows in the night.
Each breath forms a silver mist,
Nature's secrets, softly kissed.

Crystals sparkle, light confound,
Magic in the frosty ground.
Whispers call from deep within,
Icy tales of where we've been.

Footprints trace the path we've roamed,
Along the edges, softly combed.
Laughter echoes, bright and clear,
In this realm, we have no fear.

As night descends with quiet grace,
Stars emerge, we find our place.
Together in this frozen land,
Icy echoes, hand in hand.

Twilight Whispers

As the sun dips low and fades,
Colors blend in soft cascades.
Whispers dance upon the breeze,
Twilight's charm, the heart's appease.

Crickets hum a gentle song,
In the dusk, where we belong.
Shadows stretch and twilight glows,
Nature's magic, softly flows.

Stars awaken, one by one,
Nighttime's secrets just begun.
Moonlit paths invite our dreams,
Guiding us with silver beams.

In the sky, the canvas writ,
Every hue, a soundless hit.
Moments captured, softly kept,
In this hour, where dreams have crept.

As day surrenders, calm and sweet,
Hearts entwined, a soft heartbeat.
In twilight's grasp, the world stands still,
Whispers linger, time to fill.

Hushed Radiance

In the quiet of the dawn,
Golden rays, the night is gone.
Softly wrapped in morning light,
Hushed radiance, pure and bright.

Every shadow weaves a tale,
In the stillness, whispers sail.
Gentle breezes, nature's breath,
Life unfolds beyond its death.

Petals open, colors gleam,
In this moment, we shall dream.
Beneath the sky, vast and grand,
Beauty blooms across the land.

Time stands still, a sacred space,
Each heartbeat, a warm embrace.
In this hush, the world awakes,
Radiance shines, our spirit takes.

From the depths, we rise anew,
In the light, our hearts break through.
Hushed radiance holds us tight,
In the dawn's soft, golden light.

Winter's Orbit

Circling round the stars above,
Winter's breath, a tale of love.
Frosted branches twist and sway,
Underneath the moon's soft ray.

Snowflakes fall like whispered dreams,
Creating worlds in silver beams.
Each night whispers secrets old,
Winter's stories waiting to be told.

The frozen ground holds quiet grace,
In this stillness, we find our place.
Time slows down in frosty air,
Nature's beauty everywhere.

Candles flicker, shadows play,
In the heart of winter's sway.
Embers glow, a soft embrace,
As we wander, find our space.

Underneath the starry dome,
In winter's orbit, we find home.
Wrapped in warmth, together here,
Facing forward, drawing near.

Frostbound Infinity

In a world where silence reigns,
Whispers of snow weave intricate chains.
Each flake a story, soft and bright,
All dance together in the pale moonlight.

Time seems to linger, frozen in place,
Merging with shadows, an ethereal grace.
Endless horizons, where frost meets the sky,
A canvas of dreams where cold dreams lie.

The landscape sparkles, a shimmering sea,
Reflecting the wonders that nature can be.
Glistening crystals adorn every tree,
In this frostbound infinity, we long to be.

Winds carry secrets, as soft as a sigh,
While stars twinkle brightly in the midnight sky.
Each breath of the air tastes crisp and divine,
In a world where frost and magic entwine.

Boundless and tranquil, this stillness we crave,
Within frozen realms, our hearts feel so brave.
The whispers of winter will never depart,
In this frostbound infinity, we find our heart.

Heavenly Frostwork

The dawn breaks softly, a pastel hue,
As frostwork adorns the world anew.
Delicate patterns, nature's decree,
Unveiling the beauty for all to see.

Sunlight paints magic on icy streams,
Each glimmering surface reflects our dreams.
A tapestry woven with silvery thread,
Where wishes are whispered and secrets are said.

Branches are cloaked in a shimmering veil,
In this frozen wonderland, we set our sail.
Each step we take is a gentle caress,
As nature reveals her serene tenderness.

Clouds drift above, like thoughts in the night,
Carving out paths in soft morning light.
Frost flakes descend, like heavenly sighs,
Filling our hearts with tranquility's prize.

A quiet enchantment, so pure and profound,
In this heavenly frostwork, peace can be found.
Within every flake lies a glimpse of the stars,
In a world wrapped in wonder, where magic is ours.

Frozen Dreams Above

Under the gaze of the winter moon,
Dreams take flight, like whispers in June.
Crystals of ice hang from the eaves,
A tapestry woven from long-sought reprieves.

The night is draped in a silvery cloak,
In the hush of the evening, our hearts gently soak.
Stars gleam brightly, a celestial sea,
Guiding our thoughts to where we yearn to be.

Each breath leaves a trace of frosted delight,
As we wander through realms painted in white.
Frozen moments captured, etched in the air,
In this dreamlike landscape, we are laid bare.

The stillness envelops, a comforting shroud,
In this world where whispers are spoken aloud.
Hope dances lightly on the tip of a breath,
In the frozen dreams above, we find warmth in death.

With every heartbeat, the cosmos aligns,
In the symphony of ice, our spirit entwines.
We yearn for the warmth, but cherish the chill,
In frozen dreams above, we crave and fulfill.

The Silent Glitter

Snowflakes flutter like secrets set free,
Each one a promise, a gem from the sea.
They settle softly on slumbering ground,
In the silent glitter, harmony is found.

The world transforms into a canvas of light,
As shadows retreat, surrendering to night.
Every corner shines with delicate grace,
Embracing the magic that time can erase.

Footsteps are muffled, a whispering tune,
Between brightly lit stars and the watching moon.
A symphony woven from nature's own thread,
The silent glitter crests over our heads.

Across frozen ponds where reflections do play,
Memories linger in the stillness of day.
Each shard of ice, a glittering gem,
In this tranquil landscape, we feel like a hem.

As twilight approaches, the sky starts to fade,
The silent glitter blankets the glade.
In the hush of the night, we pause to admire,
The elegance frozen, our hearts set on fire.

Shattered Dreams of Winter

Whispers of frost on a cold, pale night,
Shadows dance softly, under soft moonlight.
Promises linger in the crisp, chilled air,
Yet hopes lie scattered, beyond repair.

Snowflakes descend on the dreams that once soared,
Each flake a memory, a heart that was floored.
Fractured reflections in icicles bright,
Capture the echoes of lost winter's light.

Footsteps in silence, a pathway undone,
Worn trails remind of the laughter and fun.
But time is a thief, with a heart made of stone,
Leaving the remnants of dreams overthrown.

Ghosts in the twilight, where visions once gleamed,
We walk on the borders of what we once dreamed.
Yet still there's a spark in the shadows we cast,
A glimmer of hope for a future unmasked.

In the quiet of night, let the heart softly weep,
For winter will pass, and the world will not sleep.
New dreams will awaken, with spring's gentle call,
And shatter the echoes of winter's cruel fall.

Chilled Epiphanies

In the stillness of night, clarity breathes,
Thoughts dance like leaves caught in cold, bitter wreaths.
Ice crystals forming, reflections of truth,
Reveal hidden secrets of lost, fleeting youth.

In hollowed-out spaces, where silence prevails,
Whispers of wisdom drift softly on gales.
Moments of light break the long, darkened spell,
Cold fragments of knowing, sweet stories to tell.

Frozen in time, a revelation ignites,
Paths once uncertain now glow with new sights.
Each frosted breath carries echoes of grace,
Awakening hearts in this chill-laden space.

Frost-covered windows, the world looks anew,
Every shard of clear ice holds visions so true.
Though sharp are the edges, the beauty is found,
In tangled reflections where peace can abound.

To acknowledge the cold is to cherish the fire,
And seek the warm light that we all so desire.
In the depth of the night, chilled epiphanies gleam,
Guiding us gently through winter's harsh dream.

Numbed Twinkles

Stars blink above in the frostbitten skies,
Each twinkle a whisper, a soft, muffled sigh.
Winter's deep slumber enfolds every dream,
Wrapped in a silence, lost in the gleam.

Nights stretch like shadows, cold fingers unfold,
Tales left untold in the air bitterly cold.
Eyes look for warmth in the vastness above,
But find only numbness, a longing for love.

Icicles dangle like dreams from the past,
Each sharp little point reminds us of fast.
Hopes hang in balance, like snowflakes that fall,
Torn between futures, they long for the call.

Yet in the stillness, beneath all the pain,
There flickers a light in the soft, gentle rain.
For every lost twinkle, a new one will bloom,
To chase away shadows and pierce through the gloom.

So let's breathe in deeply this chilled, quiet night,
And welcome the stars with their shimmering light.
In numbness, we find hidden wonders that soar,
Numbed twinkles above, where our hearts can explore.

Silent Frosting

A layer of white on the world softly gleams,
Silent frosting dances on delicate dreams.
Each branch wears a shimmer, each rooftop a crown,
Transforming the mundane in white velvet gown.

Footprints are muted, a hush fills the air,
Echoes of laughter now linger, a prayer.
Snow blankets whispers, the day seems to pause,
Nature holds secrets in gentle applause.

Shadows stretch longer, like fingers of night,
Veiling the world in a soft, tender light.
Where once there was chaos, now quiet prevails,
Each moment a story in silence regales.

Hearts warm in the stillness; we watch and we wait,
For spring's gentle thaw to open the gate.
But for now, we cherish this peace in the cold,
With dreams softly wrapped in the quiet, pure gold.

So let it snow softly, let the stillness seep,
Into every crevice, into every deep.
For in silent frosting, our spirits will find,
The beauty of winter, with moments entwined.

Milton Keynes UK
Ingram Content Group UK Ltd.
UKHW010231111224
452348UK00011B/666

9 789916 797129